Editor **Yudai Igarashi**
Cover **Courtney Utt**
Graphics Design **Izumi Hirayama**

Managing Editor **Annette Roman**
Editorial Director **Elizabeth Kawasaki**
Editor in Chief **Alvin Lu**
Sr. Director of Acquisitions **Rika Inouye**
Sr. VP of Marketing **Liza Coppola**
Exec. VP of Sales & Marketing **John Easum**
Publisher **Hyoe Narita**

BEYBLADE

Story & Art **Takao Aoki**
English Adaptation **Fred Burke**
Translation **Akira Watanabe**
Touch-Up & Lettering **Dave Lanphear**
Graphics & Cover Design **Andrea Rice**
Interior Design **Andrea Rice**
Editor **Ian Robertson**

© 2000 Takao AOKI/Shogakukan Inc.
© 2000 HUDSONSOFT/TAKARA
BEYBLADE logo and graphics © HUDSON SOFT/TAKARA •
BEYBLADE PROJECT • TV TOKYO. Licensed by d-rights Inc.
First published by Shogakukan Inc. in Japan as "Bakuten
Shoot Beyblade."

MEGAMAN NT WARRIOR

Story & Art **Ryo Takamisaki**
English Adaptation **Gary Leach**
Translation **Koji Goto**
Touch-Up & Lettering **Gia Cam Luc**
Graphics & Cover Design **Carolina Ugalde**
Editor **Eric Searleman**

© 2001 Ryo TAKAMISAKI/Shogakukan Inc. © CAPCOM Co.,
Ltd. ™and ® are trademarks of CAPCOM Co., Ltd. First
published by Shogakukan Inc. in Japan as "Rokkuman
Eguze."

store.viz.com

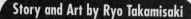

SAY WHAT?!

WHTSH

SAY WHAT?!

SAY WHAT?!

WHTSH

WHTSH

I'M NOT LIKE YOU, DEX.

I DON'T PICK ON WEAKLINGS LIKE...WELL, LIKE *GUTSMAN!*

SHU-WHAM

DIDN'T YOU TWO LISTEN TO *ANYTHING* I SAID?!

MEGAMAN, WHAT TIME IS IT?

WELL, IT'S 10:43:52 A.M...

I'M LEAVING *EARLY* TODAY, OKAY?

MS. MARI!

IF YOU *DON'T* TAKE THIS *SERIOUSLY,* I'M GOING TO REALLY HAVE TO...

HE'S NOT SURE *WHEN* HE'LL BE ABLE TO GET TIME OFF AGAIN...

SOMETHING CAME UP AT THE LABORATORY, APPARENTLY....

...ABOUT THIS LATEST COMPUTER VIRUS GOING AROUND...

Lan's Room
&
MegaMan's

I'M SORRY, LAN.

YOUR FATHER DID SEND AN E-MAIL EARLY THIS MORNING, AND....

...I TRIED TO FIND THE RIGHT TIME TO TELL YOU...

I'M...NOT REALLY DISAPPOINTED....

...

I KNEW YOU'D BE TERRIBLY DISAPPOINTED...

...AND I...

I KNEW YOU WERE REALLY LOOKING FORWARD TO THIS.

SHOOT
...

"YOU'RE
JUST A
STUPID
PROGRAM
!!"

!!

DO
YOU...
SMELL
SOME-
THING?

I MEAN
...LIKE
SOMETHING
BURNING
...

HOW
DARE
YOU
THINK
THAT
WAS
...!

WHOA!
I DON'T
MEAN
THAT!

UM...

YAI.

ZT
ZT

THE HEATING SYSTEM'S GONE *HAYWIRE*!!

Current Room Temperature :133°F

TEMPERATURE'S *ALREADY* AT...133 DEGREES ?!

IF IT CAN BE *FLUSHED*, THAT SHOULD FIX IT! THE FIRE SHOULD SUBSIDE!

ONLY ONE THING COULD BE DOING THIS - A *VIRUS* IN THE THERMO-STAT!!

AW MAN, I FORGOT! I LEFT HIM AT *HOME!!*

...

GET SET, MEGA....

I'LL JACK IN FROM THIS PANEL!

WAIT! THESE COMPUTERS ARE NET- WORKED!

I CAN CALL HIM FROM *HERE!*

NETOP: LAN HIKARI

NETNAVI: MEGAMAN

VOICE I.D. CON- FIRMED!

MEGA- MAN!

I *NEED* YOU AT SCHOOL!

MEGA- MAN, LISTEN!

HURRY UP! *COME ON!*

NOTHING! IS HE OFFLINE...?

MEGA- MAN!

FWO OOSH

MEGA- MAN!

LET IT RIP!

BEYBLADE

Story and Art by Takao Aoki

Tyson's on a mission to be the best Beyblader ever! But his enemies, the Blade Sharks, are *super* tough and they'll do anything to win! Tyson just might have what it takes to win when he busts out with a new Beyblade given to him by a mysterious stranger. Now the Blade Sharks want his new Beyblade and they're prepared to use any dirty trick to get it!

Story and Art by **Takao Aoki** 1

BASED ON THE HIT ANIME TV SERIES!

PRODUCT TIE-INS INCLUDE A TV SERIES, VIDEO GAMES, AND TOYS.

- Bimonthly
- $7.99
- Volume 12 available in Aug. 2006!

RATED A FOR ALL AGES

FROM NOW ON JUST CALL ME *BEYBLADE KING!*

THAT TYSON GUY'S REALLY GOOD.

MAYBE *TOO* GOOD! HAS HE EVER *LOST?*

HUH!?

TIKKA TEKK...

I'LL JOT THAT DOWN!

"TYSON. PERSONALITY: EGOCENTRIC. ABILITY: AVERAGE."

WHO ARE *YOU* TO DIS *ME,* HUH, CHIEF? WHADDA *YOU* KNOW ABOUT BEYBLADES!?

WHAT DO *I* KNOW? JUST ABOUT *EVERYTHING!* BEYBLADES ARE THE SUBJECT OF MY RESEARCH!

HERE YA GO, MASARU! IT'S LUCKY YOUR PRIZED BEYBLADE DIDN'T GET BROKEN.

YOU SURE DID!

OUCH! BUT I GOT IT...

GOOD OL' TYSON.

THANKS, TYSON. I OWE YOU ONE...

Y-YEAH! VERY LUCKY!

MY BEYBLADE GOT TAKEN!

HEY! COME QUICK, YOU GUYS!

GEE, KENTA! WHAT'S UP!?

GIVE IT BACK TO HIM!

THAT'S MINE!

HEY!

THIS ONE'S *MINE* NOW, BUB! THE SPOILS OF WAR! *HEH...*

TW MP

USE IT OR LOSE IT! *THAT'S* THE RULE OF THE BLADE SHARKS!

OH, YEAH? WHO SAYS, TOUGH GUY?

NO ONE'S TAKING AN BEYBLADE AROUND *HERE!*

TYSON!!

THE BLADE SHARKS!?

I'VE HEARD OF THEM! A GANG OF BEYBLADE BULLIES WHO'LL STOP AT *NOTHING* TO GET THEIR WAY!

THEIR TACTICS ARE THE *WORST!*

I WON'T LET YOU GET AWAY WITH IT!

Fwoosh

TYSON!

GUESS WE SHOULD JUST GIVE UP OUR 'BLADES *NOW...*

SO MUCH FOR US, HUH?

HUH!?

THE ONLY *WIMP* HERE IS *YOU!*

OKAY! WHO'S UP NEXT? OR HAVE YOUR SPINES ALL GONE LIMP, WIMPS!?

yikes

yikes

BLADE SHARKS

VSH

LET IT RIP!

VSH

ZANG KCHANG

KNOCK HIM OUT OF THE RING!

WHAT!?

heh

C'MON! PUSH HIM OUT!

TYSON'S BEYBLADE IS ON THE OFFENSIVE! ALL *RIGHT!*

VWSSH

ON THE OTHER HAND, THE BLADE SHARK'S BEYBLADE IS HOLDING ITS MOMENTUM.

YAY! GO!

AT FIRST GLANCE IT SEEMS LIKE TYSON HAS THE ADVANTAGE-- BUT HE'S ACTUALLY LOSING TORQUE!

...TO WIN A BEYBLADE BATTLE!

ALL IT TAKES IS THE SLIGHTEST EDGE...

SKRANG

TYSON IS GONNA LOSE!

TYSON WAS HIT JUST AS HE STARTED TO WAVER!

HOW CAN THIS BE!

KRNCH

GOTTA GET MY BEY-BLADE!

WHOOSH

I'LL FIGHT YOU ANY TIME!

IF YOU'RE SO UPSET, YOU CAN ALWAYS BATTLE FOR IT!

I'LL TAKE THAT, LOSER!

YOU JERK! GIVE IT BACK!

AFTER ALL, HOW OFTEN DO I GET TO BEAT THE PANTS OFF *ROYALTY?* SEE YA LATER, *KING!*

HA HA HA

WHAT DID YOU DO *THAT* FOR*!?*

YOU ARE TOO QUICK TO USE YOUR *FISTS!*

IF YOU ARE A *TRUE* BEYBLADER, YOU *KNOW* WHAT YOU MUST DO!

VWEE

KNSH

HEY! WAIT UP! WHO ARE YOU!?

FWSH

ZEEOOSH

WHAT A COOL BEYBLADE!

YOU OKAY? HEY!

ARE YOU ALL RIGHT, TYSON!?

THAT GUY *GAVE* THIS TO ME!?

TYSON!

I HATE TO ADMIT IT... BUT THAT GUY'S RIGHT!

THE ONLY *REAL* REVENGE... IS WITH A BEYBLADE!

FISTS WON'T DO IT!

MADE ME THINK THIS 'BLADE MIGHT HAVE SOME AMAZING SECRET. OH, WELL...

DARN. THAT GUY WAS SO *WEIRD!*

ACCORDING TO MY DEEP ANALYSIS, THERE'S NOTHING REALLY SPECIAL ABOUT THIS BEYBLADE.

OKAY, CHIEF! WHAT'S THE DEAL?

ZWIRRRR

HUH!? THERE'S A BLUE DRAGON CARVED IN THE CENTER.

...WHEN I LOOK AT THIS DRAGOON, I FEEL *POWER* RISE UP INSIDE OF ME!

I'M FINE! IT'S JUST ODD...

WHAT'S WRONG, TYSON!?

GWRR

LET'S GO, DRAGOON!

WE'RE GONNA TAKE CARE OF THAT BULLY ONCE AND FOR ALL!

SKRRSH

I'M GOING TO NAME THIS ONE *DRAGOON*, DUDE!

TAKE A LOOK AT THE DATA.

WHY WOULD YOU SAY *THAT*!?

WHAT?!

NO WAY!

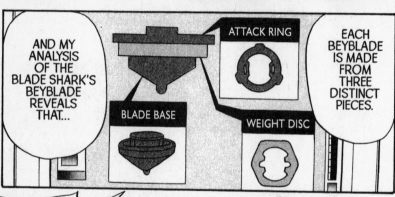

AND MY ANALYSIS OF THE BLADE SHARK'S BEYBLADE REVEALS THAT...

ATTACK RING

BLADE BASE

WEIGHT DISC

EACH BEYBLADE IS MADE FROM THREE DISTINCT PIECES.

IN OTHER WORDS, WITH YOUR PRESENT ATTACK POWER, YOU'LL RUN OUT OF STAMINA IN THE LONG RUN!

HEAVY METAL ALLOY GIVES IT BETTER DEFENSE AND ENDURANCE!

...ITS WEIGHT DISC HAS BEEN MODIFIED!

GHAK

THAT'S WHY I PLANNED AHEAD! CHECK IT OUT!

THEN WE JUST HAVE TO INCREASE THE TORQUE AND USE A RAPID ATTACK STRATEGY!

VWRRSH

SEE?! IT'S SPINNING A LOT FASTER THAN BEFORE!

LET IT RIP!

SVRRRR

LONG LIVE THE KING!

I PUT TWO SHOOTER RACKS END TO END!

SHOOTER RACK

SHOOTER

SO IT'S NOT ENOUGH, HUH? HOW MUCH DO WE NEED TO INCREASE IT BY!?

BUT IT'S STILL ONLY TWICE THE TORQUE THAT IT WAS BEFORE.

GET OFF MY CASE, WILL YA!

YOU REALLY PUT THAT LITTLE BRAIN TO USE!

FOUR TIMES MORE!? BUT *HOW*...?

LEMME SEE... BY **FOUR TIMES!** THAT WOULD BEAT HIM!

STILL FULL OF THE OLD CHILDISH ENTHUSIASM, TYSON!

THAT'S *NOT* WHAT I'M SAYING...

THERE'S NO WAY! I CAN'T MAKE THE SHOOTER RACK ANY LONGER!

MY ARM'S TOO SHORT!

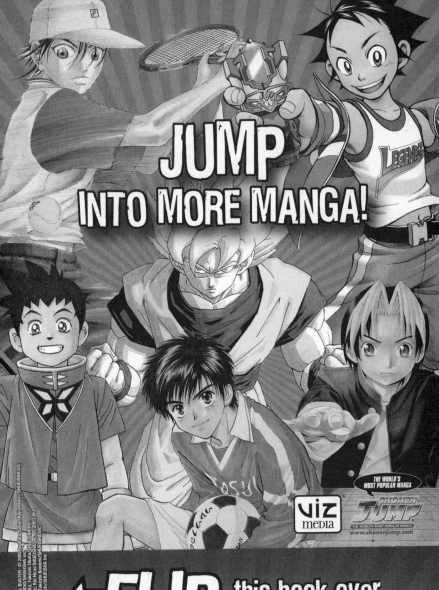

WAIT!
THERE'S MORE!!

⇦FLIP this book over for a sneak peek at BEYBLADE and MEGAMAN NT WARRIOR!

WAS THAT SUPPOSED TO BE YOUR SECOND SERVE?

HEY...

YOU IDIOTS, HE JUST GOT LUCKY!

THAT WAS AS FAST AS SASABE'S FIRST SERVE!

WHAAITT, YOU GOTTA BE KIDDING !?

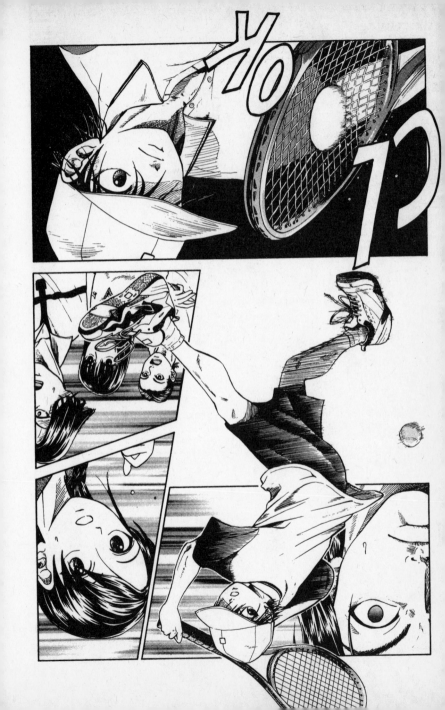

WAS THAT TOO FAST?

YOU WANT MY SECOND SERVE?

GA HA HA...

HEH, LOOKS LIKE HE'S SCARED.

NO, NOT TOO FAST...

WOW, HIS FIRST SERVE WAS ABOUT 100 MILES AN HOUR!

HE'S GOING ALL OUT AGAINST THAT LITTLE KID! BRUTAL!!

HA HA HA

THIS... THIS IS REALLY DANGEROUS!

BA-BUMP

BA-BUMP

BAMMM

BA

I'M NOT GOING EASY JUST BECAUSE YOU'RE A LITTLE KID!

ALL RIGHT THEN...

SKERK

IT'S TOO SLOW!

HEY HEY,
HE'S
GOING
TO GO
AGAINST
SASABE
FOR
REAL!!

GET HIM
!!
KICK
HIS ASS!

HEY
KID!
LOOKS
LIKE
YOU'RE
GONNA
REGRET
THIS.
YOU'VE
GOTTA
LEARN
THE
HARD
WAY.

THAT'S
NICE.

SKREET
SKREET

SOME-
THING
TOTALLY
HORRIBLE
HAS
HAPPENED!

TENNIS GROUNDS

PRACTICE COURTS

i'LL TEACH YOU SOME TENNIS !!

IF YOU DO....

GULP

FSHOOO

DID YOU REMEM- BER THE GRIP?

HEY...

AWWW, POOR BABY!

HEH HEH HEH

BUH-BYEE!

AND DON'T FORGET IT!

AHA HA HA HA

GOT IT? YOU CAN'T WIN TENNIS JUST BY MEMORIZING THE FACTS!

DOKK

DOKK

BUMP

EEK!

WHA!? YOU GOT YOUR @#$%* JUICE ON ME!

SWAK

UNLIKE BABY HERE, I HAVE A MATCH BEFORE THE FINALS!

NOW MY CLOTHES ARE ALL STICKY! WHAT AM I SUPPOSED TO DO, BRAT?

I... I'M SORRY...

SMIRK

WATCH OUT !!

AHH !!

YOU GOT ANOTHER 10 YEARS BEFORE A BRAT LIKE YOU CAN TEACH ME ABOUT TENNIS.

STOP

OH NO! IT'S THE HIGH-SCHOOL-ERS FROM BEFORE...!

OOOH! LOOKS LIKE HE LOST ALREADY— ALL PACKED UP AND READY TO GO HOME!

HEY.

ISN'T THAT THE BRAT FROM BEFORE?

I'M SORRY, I DIDN'T HAVE ANY CHANGE... AND NOW YOU'RE TREATING ME.

CLUNK

UH, GRANDMA, I'M GOING TO LOOK OVER THERE, OKAY!!

YOU ARE SUCH A STRANGE GIRL.

BE CAREFUL!!

SCREEE

IF YOU'RE LATE FOR A TOURNAMENT...

WHAT HAPPENS?

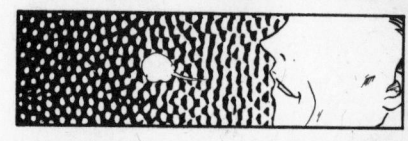

WHAA?!

SLAM

WELL, YOU'RE DEFAULTED--

DISQUALIFIED!

LET'S SEE HOW THE PRINCE OF TENNIS IS DOING.

WELL THEN
.....

OH!?

RUSTLE

C'MON AND GET IN! I'LL DRIVE!

SUMIRE RYUZAKI (58) SEISHUN ACADEMY MIDDLE SCHOOL

WHAAAAATTT!!!?

WHAT ARE YOU TALKING ABOUT, SAKUNO? WHERE'S YOUR SENSE OF DIRECTION?

HUH...? ISN'T IT BY THE SOUTH GATE?

KAKINOK- IZAKA TENNIS GARDEN... ...IS OUT THE NORTH GATE.

BUT THERE'S SOMEONE I WANT TO SEE... THE SON OF A STUDENT OF MINE...

TODAY'S TOURNAMENT IS GOING TO BE NOTHING BUT LOW LEVEL MATCHES...

UH... UM, GRAND- MA...

VRROOM

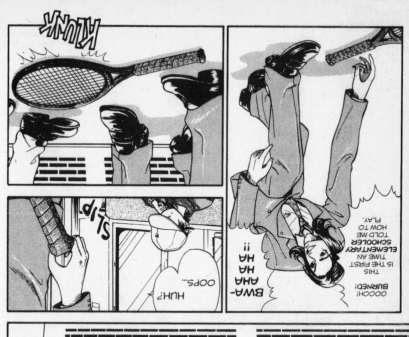

OOOOH! BURNED!

THIS IS THE FIRST TIME AN ELEMENTARY SCHOOLER TOLD ME HOW TO PLAY.

BWA-AHA HA HA !!

HUH? OOPS...

SLIP...

KIUUNK

KYATTA

KYATTA

....SO WHICH WAY?

ARE YOU GOING TO ENTER THE TOURNAMENT? THIS IS THE FIRST TIME I'VE BEEN TO A TENNIS MATCH SO...

UM, YEAH, I'M GOING THERE TOO.

G-GO STRAIGHT OUT THE SOUTH GATE, YOU CAN'T MISS IT.

BLUSH

ER, I'M REALLY SORRY, I...

30 MINUTES LATER...

THE SOUTH EXIT.... THANKS.

SO HIS NAME IS RYOMA....

RYOMA.E

HEEEYYY SAKUNO!

I'M SO SORRY!

TICKET GATES →

TICKET VENDING MACHINES

OH GRANDMA, YOU'RE LATE!

OH! THIS IS MY STOP TOO!

SHE INVITED ME TO THE TENNIS TOURNAMENT WITH HER, BUT AT THIS RATE I'M GOING TO BE LATE...

GRANDMA ISN'T HERE...

TURN

ACK, H-HE'S LOOKING THIS WAY !?

HUH!? IT'S THAT BOY!

HEY... WHICH WAY IS THE KAKINOKIZAKA TENNIS GARDEN?

KYATTA

KYATTA

OOOOH! BURNED!

THIS IS THE FIRST TIME AN **ELEMENTARY SCHOOLER** TOLD ME HOW TO PLAY.

BWA-AHA HA HA !!

HUH?

OOPS...

SLIP

KLUNK

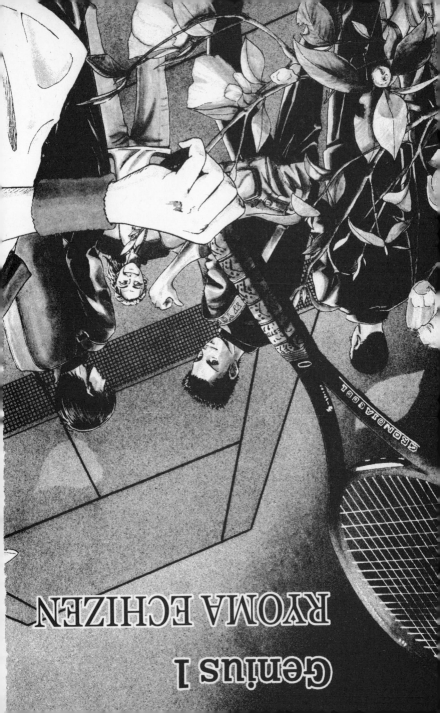

A tennis prodigy's journey in leading his team all the way to the Nationals!

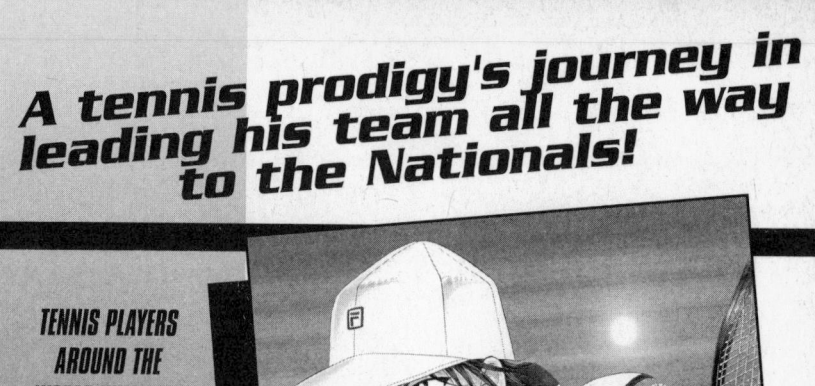

TENNIS PLAYERS
AROUND THE
WORLD WILL LOVE
THIS MANGA!

ADAPTED INTO A
JAPANESE ANIME
SERIES AND
VIDEO GAMES!

- Volume 16 available in November 2006!
- $7.95
- Bimonthly

SHONEN JUMP MANGA

Story & Art by **Takeshi Konomi**

THE PRINCE OF TENNIS

volume 12

Nobody ever thought that a 7th grader could be a starter on the school tennis team. With a formidable squad made up of skilled and experienced upperclassmen, a small 12-year-old player just didn't seem to be a threat. Little do they know that The Prince of Tennis Ryoma Echizen is the much-needed secret weapon who could lead Seishun Academy all the way to the Nationals!

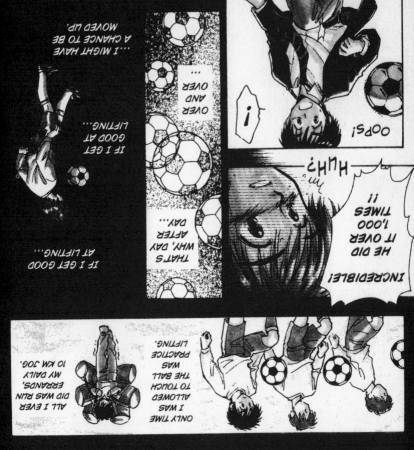

HE'S AN EXCEPTIONAL PLAYER. MUSASHINOMORI EVEN TRIED TO RECRUIT HIM-- IT'S A MYSTERY WHY HE CAME HERE INSTEAD.

REALLY?

GOOD EYE, SHŌ! YOU'VE ALREADY SPOTTED TATSUYA!

OH, YOU MEAN, MIZUNO? HE'S TATSUYA MIZUNO OF SECOND YEAR.

HE'S A MID-FIELDER, BUT HE CAN HANDLE ANY POSITION.

YŪSUKE, WHO'S THAT INCREDIBLE GUY?

... THAT'S LIKE A COMPLETELY DIFFERENT WORLD FROM US--

YOU'RE FROM MUSASHI-NOMORI ...

POLITE? BUT, YOU...

AND PLEASE, YOU DON'T HAVE TO BE SO POLITE TO ME.

HEY YŪSUKE !!

BUT I'M NOT. I'M --

GOTTA GO, SHŌ.

QUIT GOOFING OFF. GET TO WORK.

BYE

AH ...

OH ...

YÛSUKE
OF
SECOND
YEAR.

WHAT'S
YOUR
NAME?

ER
...

YES?

OOPS

HE'S
MUSASHI-
NOMORI
GOOD.

MUCH
BETTER
THAN THE
OTHERS.

HE'S
GOOD.

WHMP

YAYYYY

HOW DO I TELL
THEM I WAS
JUST IN THE
THIRD TEAM?

READ
THIS
WAY

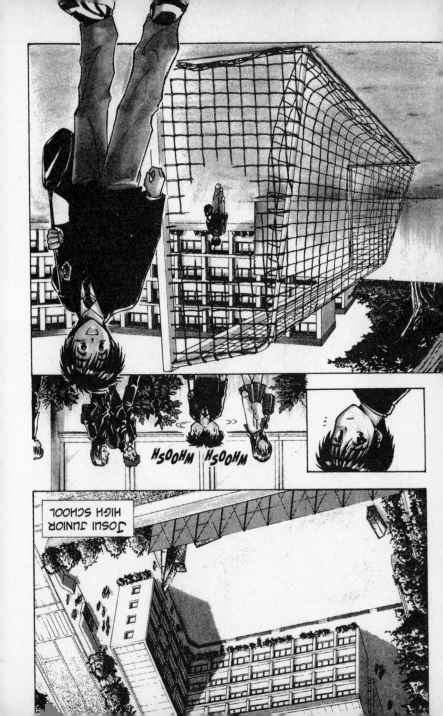

WHOOSH WHOOSH

JOSUI JUNIOR HIGH SCHOOL

SNIFF - HOW WONDERFUL TO WAKE UP TO THE DELICIOUS SMELL OF BREAKFAST. ♡
UGH!
YUCHH
KISS ♥
BUT, YOU KNOW WHAT REALLY MAKES ME HAPPY ?
THAT SMILE OF YOURS ...
HEY! YOU'RE STILL SLEEPING. WAKE UP!
WHUMP
UN-HHH
HUH
WHAT ARE YOU DOING ?!
MY FACE IS MY BUSINESS. HOW COULD YOU?
HEY, IT'S YOUR FAULT, BRO. YOU'RE THE ONE WHO MISTOOK ME AS ONE OF YOUR CUSTOMERS!
HUH ... SHŌ ?
SHAME ON YOU.
OH, YEAH, RIGHT.
I FORGOT IT'S ONLY BEEN A WEEK SINCE YOU GOT HERE.

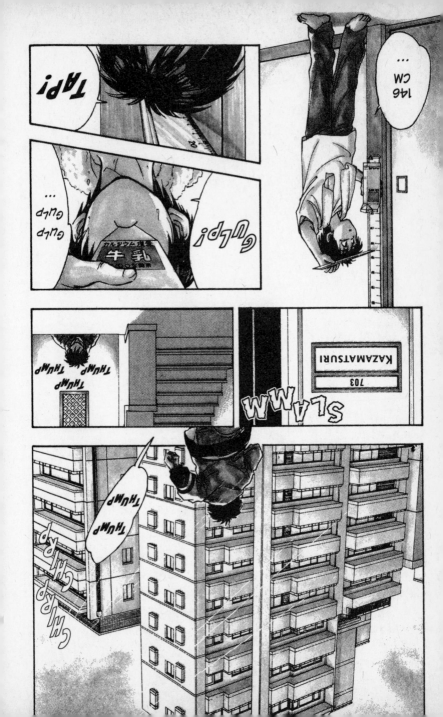

● INTRODUCTION ●

SOCCER IS A SPORT IN WHICH THE PLAYER'S TEAM STEALS THE BALL FROM THE OPPONENT'S TEAM THEN PASSES IT FROM PLAYER TO PLAYER UNTIL IT IS SHOT INTO THE OTHER TEAM'S GOAL. IT MAY SOUND EASY, BUT YOUR OPPONENTS WILL INTERFERE, MAKING IT DIFFICULT TO SCORE.

TO MAKE A GOAL, TEAMS ESTABLISH POSITIONS, INITIATE PASSES, SET UP COMPLICATED FORMATIONS AND TRY TO OUT-MANEUVER OPPONENTS.

THESE DAYS, THE PLAYERS, EXCLUDING GOALKEEPERS, CHANGE POSITIONS SO RAPIDLY AND CONSTANTLY THAT IT'S OFTEN HARD TO KEEP TRACK OF WHO IS POSITIONED WHERE. SINCE, UNLIKE BASEBALL, PLAYERS' POSITIONS ARE NOT FIXED, IT IS NOT NECESSARY TO KNOW WHERE THEY ARE AS YOU WATCH THEM PLAY. ALL YOU NEED TO DO IS KEEP IN MIND WHICH PLAYER TAKES WHAT POSITION WITHIN A FORMATION SUCH AS 4-4-2 OR 3-5-2.

BEYOND THAT, FOCUS ON FIGURING OUT HOW TO GAIN POINTS AND WHEN TO STEAL THE BALL. YOU MUST NOT ONLY WATCH THE GOAL BUT ALSO THE PROCESS OF GETTING THERE.

YOU WILL ENJOY SOCCER IF YOU CAN UNDERSTAND, AS AN EXAMPLE, THAT JOE'S GOAL WAS THE RESULT OF YAMAGUCHI'S PASS-CUT, OR THAT THE GOAL WAS POSSIBLE BECAUSE OF THE LAST PASS.

SOCCER ALLOWS PLAYERS TO USE ANY PART OF THEIR BODIES EXCEPT FOR THEIR HANDS. USING VARIOUS PARTS OF A PLAYER'S LEG, APPLYING DIVERSE INTENSITIES AS WELL AS DIFFERENT ANGLES, ALLOWS FOR A GREAT MANY WAYS TO PASS A BALL. ADDING BOTH LEGS AND FEET AS WELL AS YOUR HEAD, AND YOU'LL FIND IT IMPOSSIBLE TO COUNT HOW MANY WAYS A PLAYER CAN MAKE A PASS. ISN'T IT ALREADY EXCITING TO THINK ABOUT IT?

--TATSUYA WATANABE (WINNING RUN)

DID IT!

TWINK

DON'T LET GO OF THE DREAM!!

BELIEVE!

NEVER HESITATE!

BELIEVE IN YOUR OWN STRENGTH!!

IF YOU BELIEVE, THEN YOUR DREAMS ...

WILL COME TRUE WITHOUT FAIL! ...

NO MATTER THE SITUATION...

...FIGHT INSTEAD OF RUNNING AWAY!

VICTORY
OFFENSE AND DEFENSE FROM THE 40 DEGREE.
DRAW
IT'S BEEN FOUR YEARS SINCE DORHA.
FRANCE
STAGE.1
BATTLE WHERE DREAMS ARE AT STAKE.
BREAK THROUGH
-BREAK THROUGH THE WALL-
EMBARRASSMENT
DEFEAT
DESPAIR
ASIA PRELIMINARY FINALS

When the whistle blows... get ready for action!

MANGA FOR SOCCER PLAYERS & FANS!

INSPIRED A HIT ANIME SERIES!

- Volume 14 available in November 2006!
- $7.99

Banned from his school's soccer team for being too short, Shô Kazamatsuri decides there's only one thing left to do: switch schools! But even a change in scenery doesn't help the David Beckham wannabe. On campus, he is mistakenly introduced to everyone as a hotshot soccer player. When the truth is revealed, Shô drops out of school to practice on his own.

Alone, the spunky teenager must work twice as hard to make his dreams come true. He wants to play soccer so bad he's willing to hustle day and night to make it happen.

Packed with action, humor and teenage kicks, *Whistle!* is a must-read for dreamers (and soccer fans) of all ages!

OR DO YOU WANT TO BRAG ABOUT KILLING THE MONSTERS?

SO ARE YOU FIGHTING FOR MONEY?

THAT'S NOT TRUE!

WE CAN'T CALL... WHAT WE DO... JUSTICE.

...THAT'S TRUE, BUT...

YOU'RE WORKING HARD FOR THE SAKE OF THE VILLAGERS AND PEOPLE AROUND THE WORLD!!

I DON'T THINK SO!

THAT'S WHAT'S CALLED JUSTICE!!

DON'T YOU KNOW?

SHEEN

...I WANNA BE COOL LIKE YOU GUYS, ZENON!

YEAH! ZENON WARRIORS ARE THE BUSTERS OF JUSTICE, GETTING RID OF THE VANDELS AND PROTECTING HUMANS, RIGHT?

I WANNA BE A BUSTER LIKE THAT!!

...LIKE US?

YOU'VE SEEN THE WAY THE VILLAGERS LOOK AT US, HAVEN'T YOU? WE RISK OUR LIVES EVERY DAY, BUT NOBODY LIKES US.

YOU WON'T LAST LONG IDOLIZING THE JOB OR THINKING IT'S ALL FUN.

TO BE HONEST, IT'S NOT ALL THAT COOL.

JUSTICE... HOO BOY...

IT'S UNDER-STANDABLE.

ALTHOUGH OUR ENEMIES AREN'T HUMAN, WE AREN'T TOO DIFFERENT FROM ASSASSINS.

IN A WAY, WE'RE TREATED LIKE THE VANDELS.

BEET, KILLING VANDELS AND MONSTERS IS A BUSTER'S JOB. SIMPLE AS THAT.

YOU IDIOT! YOU GET THE FEWEST PROMOTION POINTS FROM THE BITING CLAMS!!

SO HOW MANY PROMOTION POINTS DO I GET FROM THIS ONE?

AM I UP TO LEVEL 5 OR SOMETHING LIKE THAT?

THANKS!

I DIDN'T EXPECT YOU TO GIVE ME ADVICE, ZENON!!

...!

HUH

I'LL SURPRISE YOU BY GETTING STRONGER WHILE YOU GUYS ARE STILL IN THE VILLAGE!!

WELL, NONETHE-LESS, I'LL DO MY BEST!

...A LONGER ROAD THAN I EXPECTED, HUH?

...

YOU'LL BE LUCKY TO REACH LEVEL 3 EVEN AFTER YOU KILL OFF A HUNDRED OF THEM.

WHY DO YOU WANT TO BECOME A BUSTER SO MUCH?

IT'S BE-CAUSE...

WELL? HOW COME?

...

HUH?

BY "FIGHTING THREE DAYS AND NIGHTS," HUH?

YOU DON'T GIVE UP, DO YOU?

HOLD THE NECK OF THE SPEAR AND, USING THE POINT, CUT THE MOUTH OFF THE SHELL FROM BEHIND!

IT'S NOT AS PAINFUL AS BEFORE!!

AHH... HE'S RIGHT!

PLOP

SLICE

SU SU

IT'S THE FIRST TIME I EVER DEFEATED A MONSTER!

I-- I DID IT!!

I DID IT!!

YIPPEE!!

SLOSH

SLOSH

SLOSH

IF YOU TIGHTEN YOUR MUSCLES, THE TEETH WILL SINK FURTHER.

LOOSEN UP FIRST!

LOOSEN UP!

...!

BUT—

BUT—

HOW CAN— IT HURTS LIKE CRAZY!

I'M TELLING YOU, YOU'RE BETTER OFF NOT BECOMING A BUSTER!!

IF YOU AGREE NOT TO BECOME ONE... ...I'LL HELP YOU OUT!

N-NO!!

NEVER!!

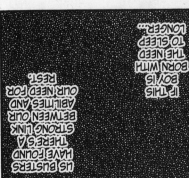

AH, BUT HOW TIRE-SOME....

IT'S THE LEAST I CAN DO.

YOU ALWAYS LET US STAY AT YOUR PLACE, EVERY TIME WE COME TO THE VILLAGE. IF YOU DIDN'T, WE'D HAVE TO CAMP OUT.

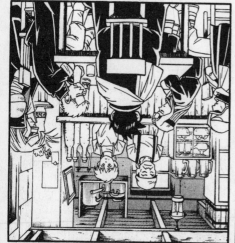

THANKS A LOT....

...LAIO.

LET ME CHECK UP ON HIM A BIT....

THUD

...

I MEANT TO RAISE THAT BOY TO LEAD A NORMAL LIFE, BUT...

I'M SORRY, ZENON.

IF A MONSTER ATTACKED HIM WHILE HE WAS ASLEEP, HE'D BE IN REAL TROUBLE.

RIGHT?

I'M NOT SO SURE! AFTER FIXING THAT ROOF, HE FELL ASLEEP WHILE HE WAS TAKING A BATH AND SLEPT THERE ALL DAY.

BY THE TIME HE WOKE UP, HIS SKIN WAS TOTALLY WRINKLED.

IT'S ADVAN-TAGEOUS TO BE ABLE TO STAY ACTIVE FOR A LONG TIME WHEN PURSUING AN ENEMY OR GOING ON AN ADVENTURE...

HMPH, IN A WAY, THAT'S PERFECT FOR A BUSTER.

WHEN ICICLE BATS PUT HOLES IN THE ROOF OF THE INN, HE FIXED IT IN THREE DAYS ON HIS OWN.

HE'D PLAY OR DO CHORES FOR THREE DAYS STRAIGHT.

HE'S UP FOR THREE DAYS AND THEN SLEEPS FOR A WHOLE DAY... HE'S BEEN LIKE THAT FOR A LONG TIME. IT'S HOW HE'S BUILT, I GUESS.

READ THIS WAY

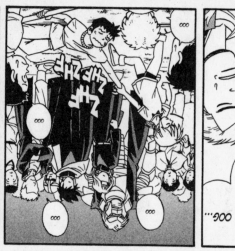

THUD

I'M... HAVING... AN IMPORTANT CONVER- SATION...

HE'S A NEW 006.... A NEW KIND OF WEAPON, ALL RIGHT....

POALA...

PO...

READ THIS WAY

TH- THAT MEANS....

...

THEY'RE NOT THE KIND OF MONSTERS THAT COME INTO BEING NATURALLY.

THIRTY IRON RHINOS.... THEY TRIED TO OPEN THE GATE.

H-HOW WAS IT, ZENON?

HEE HEE.... THE ONLY FRIENDLY LOCAL IS THE "GATE," HUH?

BUSINESS AS USUAL.

SHHK

THANK YOU.... THEY ALMOST BROKE THROUGH.... THANK YOU....

NO PROBLEM AT ALL!

"...the Century of Dark- ness..."

People call this seemingly endless era...

GO GO GO GO GOON

NOOO

Hidden in darkness, one day they appeared on the surface of the EARTH, multiplying monsters and destroying the peace and order of human society. Years have passed since that day.

Vandels!! In this story, that's what we call evil creatures with magical powers.

ZENON

"...ARE THE VANDELS!

"...THE BUSTERS' TRUE ENEMIES...

THAT'S RIGHT, AFTER ALL...

ALSIDE

...

BLUEZAM

OUR JOB IS TO DESTROY THOSE WHO CONTROL THE MON-STERS.

CRUSS

THESE MONSTERS ARE NOTHING BUT THE EVIL SERVANTS THEY PRODUCE FOR FUN...

LAIO

DON'T FEAR US JUST BECAUSE WE FINISHED AN EASY JOB LIKE THAT.

READ THIS WAY ►►

BEET
THE VANDEL BUSTER

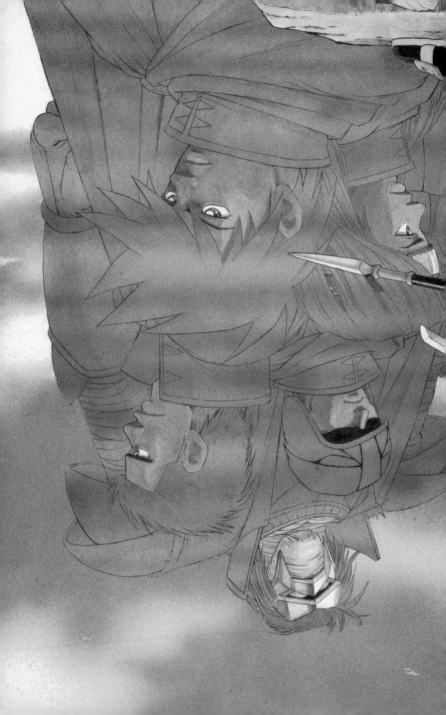

Chapter 1 – The Boy Rises!

AS I'VE SAID TO YOU MANY TIMES, ONCE YOU'RE BRANDED, YOU CAN'T GO BACK TO A NORMAL CAREER.

...SURE YOU ABOUT THIS, REALLY... BEET..?

GCHAK

...OKAY WITH THAT?

YOU'RE...

VZ VZ VZ

STARTING TODAY... I'M GONNA BE A VANDEL BUSTER!!!

TA-DA

ooo

GULP

ER... YUP! OF COURSE!

I'VE ALREADY MADE UP MY MIND!!

SHFF

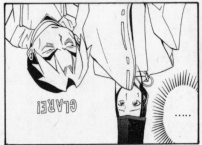

MAYBE YOU SHOULD GO SEE THE SCHOOL NURSE.

I-I THINK I'M OKAY.

ARE YOU OKAY, HIKARU?

You must have felt my intense sorrow when I heard that I would be unable to play Go.

.....

HIKARU! ARE YOU OKAY?!

huf huf

Sploooop!

WHAT'D YOU DO TO ME?!

Nothing! I didn't do anything!

gasp

SPLURP!

UGHH...

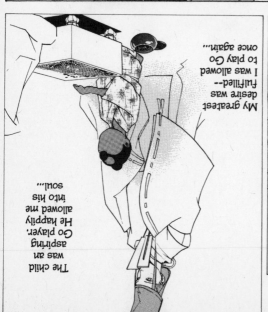

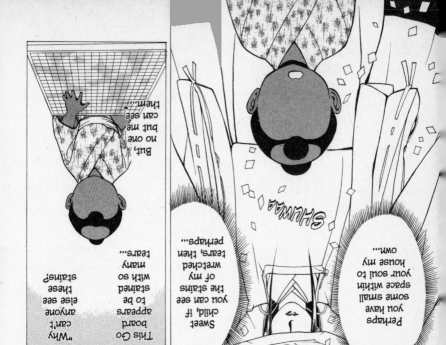
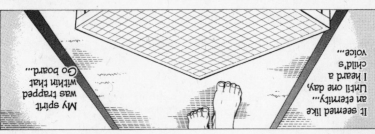

WHAT IS SHONEN JUMP?

The World of **SHONEN JUMP** is the birthplace of manga sensations Beet, Ichigo and Shô, as well as continuing hits *RUROUNI KENSHIN, SHAMAN KING, YU-GI-OH!, DRAGON BALL Z* and *THE PRINCE OF TENNIS*. Originating in Japan, each issue of *Weekly Shonen Jump* and *Monthly Shonen Jump* carries the decades-long tradition of Japanese comics propelled by vibrant art and intriguing storylines. Now that VIZ has brought the **SHONEN JUMP** magazine to the U.S., American readers can discover what millions of manga fans already know: no other comics anthology packs more action and adventure between its covers.

The real action starts in SHONEN JUMP MAGAZINE!
Subscribe now at www.shonenjump.com

WHAT IS SHONEN JUMP MANGA?

SHONEN JUMP manga is the future of manga —
it's the voice of the most exciting titles making the leap from
Japan to the U.S.

Each manga title has the unique style and voice of its artist/creator. All of the manga are presented in the right-to-left format just as they are in Japan. This format allows the panels to be displayed as the artists intended, and adds authenticity and fun to the reader's experience.

So brace yourself for an amazing adventure in **ALL AGES SNEAK PEEK**. Here's a sample of the most intense action, nail-biting cliffhangers and coolest characters around. You're about to JUMP headfirst into the world of manga. Enjoy!

THE WORLD'S MOST POPULAR MANGA

SHONEN JUMP™

Editor **Yudai Igarashi**
Cover **Courtney Utt**
Graphics Design **Izumi Hirayama**

Managing Editor **Frances E. Wall**
Editorial Director **Elizabeth Kawasaki**
VP & Editor in Chief **Yumi Hoashi**
Sr. Director of Acquisitions **Rika Inouye**
Sr. VP of Marketing **Liza Coppola**
Exec. VP of Sales & Marketing **John Easum**
Publisher **Hyoe Narita**

DRAGON BALL Z
Story & Art **Akira Toriyama**
English Adaptation **Gerard Jones**
Translation **Lillian Olsen**
Touch-Up & Lettering **Wayne Truman**
Graphics & Cover Design **Sean Lee**
Editor **Jason Thompson**

LEGENDZ
Art **Makoto Haruno**
Story **Rin Hirai**
English Adaptation **Shaenon K. Garrity**
Translation **Akira Watanabe**
Touch-Up Art & Lettering **Susan Daigle-Leach**
Graphics & Cover Design **Sean Lee**
Editor **Yuki Takagaki**

HIKARU NO GO
Story **Yumi Hotta**
Art **Takeshi Obata**
Translation &
English Adaptation **Andy Nakatani**
English Script Consultant **Janice Kim (3 Dan)**
Touch-Up Art & Lettering **Adam Symons**
Graphics & Cover Design **Sean Lee**
Editor **Livia Ching**

BEET THE VANDEL BUSTER
Story **Riku Sanjo**
Art **Koji Inada**
English Adaptation **Shaenon K. Garrity**
Translation **Naomi Kokubo**
Touch-Up & Lettering **Mark McMurray**
Graphics & Cover Design **Sean Lee & Andrea Rice**
Editor **Pancha Diaz**

THE PRINCE OF TENNIS
Story & Art **Takeshi Konomi**
English Adaptation **Gerard Jones**
Translation **Joe Yamazaki**
Touch-Up Art & Lettering **Andy Ristaino**
Graphics & Cover Design **Sean Lee**
Editor **Michelle Pangilinan**

WHISTLE!
Story & Art **Daisuke Higuchi**
English Adaptation **Marv Wolfman**
Translation **Naomi Kokubo**
Touch-Up Art & Lettering **Jim Keefe & Mark Griffin**
Graphics & Cover Design **Sean Lee**
Editor **Eric Searleman**

ALL AGES Recommended for any age group.

VIZ media
www.viz.com

THE WORLD'S MOST POPULAR MANGA
SHONEN JUMP
www.shonenjump.com

SCIENCE FICTION MARTIAL ARTS ACTION!

DBZ:05 • An Unexpected Strength

Akira Toriyama

鳥山明 BIRD STUDIO

YOU'LL STAY IN HERE!

THE BLOOD OF *SAIYANS* RUNS THROUGH YOU !!

STOP BAWLING, CHILD!

WAAA WAAA

BLANG.

STRANGE...

KCH

AN ALERT...?

BUT...

P!!!P

--MM ?

...THE NEEDS OF THE BODY MUST BE MET.

NEXT...

AND CLOSE!! WHERE?!

POWER 710 !!

WHAT ?!

THAT... INFANT ?!

PI PI PI!..

P!!!!!

...THIS IS NO TIME TO MAL-FUNCTION!

BLASTED TECHNOLOGY...

WE'D BETTER START GOING *LOWER*--

WE'RE CLOSE!!

...AN OPPONENT'S POSITION... AND HIS POWER!!

HE HOLDS A DEVICE THAT REVEALS...

WHAT?!

IT SHALL MAKE NO DIFFERENCE!!

...THERE'S NOTHING T' DO BUT *HIT HIM HEAD ON!!*

IN THAT CASE...

Y'MEAN... HE KNOWS...?

...THAT WE ARE COMING? YES.

WHAT AILS THIS DEVICE...?

POWER 710...

--AGAIN!

PI PI!!

A NEW READING...

PI PI!!

--INCOMING QUICKLY!

AND HOW WOULD HE FIND ME...?

BUT WOULD HE *DARE* TO CHALLENGE ME AGAIN, KNOWING HE HAS NO HOPE?

POWERS 322 AND 334!

ONE... NO, *TWO* OF THEM...

I NEEDN'T KEEP *IT* ANY--

THIS WORTHLESS GADGET...

ONE HAS KAKARROT'S POWER... EXACTLY.

--IT CAN'T BE!!

!!

IT IS HIM--!!

FOR A CHILD, EVEN THE CHILD OF A *SAIYAN*, TO HAVE A POWER LEVEL OF 710--

CAN IT BE THE SCOPE IS *NOT* BROKEN ??

TMP

TMP

SHH
H
H

YOU'VE FOUND A COMMON CAUSE.

I SEE.

AND HOW DID YOU FIND *ME?*

WE *DID.* THAT'S ALL.

FINE. THEN LET'S TRY ANOTHER QUESTION...

WHY DID YOU WANT TO FIND ME?

GIVE ME MY *SON*!

THEN YOU STILL REFUSE TO AFFIRM YOUR SAIYAN BIRTH BY JOINING US?

TO TAKE BACK MY *SON*!!

WHY DO YOU *THINK*!?

HOW CAN A *SAIYAN* BE SUCH A *FOOL*?

REALLY, KAKARROT... I EXPECTED SUCH BETTER THINGS OF YOU.

I DON'T *HAVE* A BROTHER!

EVEN IF IT MEANS DISOBEYING YOUR OWN BROTHER?

SURELY YOU DON'T IMAGINE THAT EVEN THE TWO OF YOU TOGETHER CAN DEFEAT *ME*...?

DNG

RADITZ... YOU TALK TOO MUCH.

FWA

AS ARE YOU, BOY...

PICCOLO... YOU WERE ARMORED, TOO?

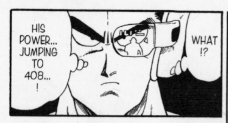
HIS POWER... JUMPING TO 408... !

WHAT!?

AND I HAVE NOT FELT SO LIGHT IN A LONG WHILE...

LOOKS LIKE WE'VE BOTH BEEN TRAINING HARD!

WELL, WELL...

...THAT *THIS* TIME, YOU'RE ON *MY* SIDE.

WELL, I'M JUST GLAD...

AND KAKARROT... UP TO 416...!

THIS...IS GONNA BE A *FIGHT!*

WA HA HA HA !!!

YOU THINK THAT MAKES A DIFFERENCE ?!

HUH ?!

YOU'LL *STILL* BE NO MATCH FOR *ME* !!

ADD *HUNDREDS* MORE DEGREES, THE *BOTH* OF YOU!!

...BUT IDIOCY HAS NO PLACE ON A SAIYAN MISSION, KAKARROT.

YOUTH I MIGHT FORGIVE...

...THEN YOU'RE NO FIGHTER!

IF YOU THINK POWER IS EVERYTHING...

YOU WILL DIE!!!!

YOU ARE A SHAME TO OUR RACE!!

PM

BWA

WELL. YOUR DEFENSES AREN'T BAD.

...YET HIS BLOWS STRUCK OUR **BACKS** !

HE CHARGED FROM THE FORE...

SO FAST I CAN HARDLY **BELIEVE** IT!!

HE... HE'S **FAST** !!

...AS I INCREASE THE POWER OF MY ATTACKS.

THAT WILL KEEP YOU ALIVE A FEW MORE MINUTES...

HIS STRENGTH'S IN HIS TAIL...BUT HOW DO WE GET TO IT...?

HE SHOWED NO SUCH POWER AS *THIS* BEFORE...

...ARE *BOTH* MY SUPERIOR IN STRENGTH.

THE OTHER SAIYANS... MY TWO PARTNERS...

...OH, ONE MORE THING. SHOULD YOU STILL HOPE TO *WIN*, YOU SHOULD KNOW...

NEXT: A NEW KIND OF FEAR!

Legendz: It's more than just a game!

FROM THE CREATORS OF TAMAGOTCHI!

A VIDEO GAME, TRADING CARDS AND AN ANIME SERIES MADE IN JAPAN!

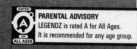

- All 4 volumes now available!
- $7.99

SHONEN JUMP GRAPHIC NOVEL

Art by MAKOTO HARUNO
(Original Concept · WiZ 2003)
Story by RIN HIRAI

volume 1

In the world of "Legendz," mythical creatures like mermaids, dragons and werewolves actually do exist. Called "Legendz," these creatures are trained by their human masters to play the ultimate role-playing game of the same name. At Ryudo Elementary, the students are busily preparing to "battle" it out in the school's Legendz tournament in hopes of winning the Golden Soul Figure, which houses a powerful but unknown Legendz. Perky Ririko Yasuhara and the school bully, Hosuke Dekai, are among the top contenders, but now there's a new kid at school who's rumored to be way too into the popular game....

HAVE YOU HEARD?

THERE'S A GAME THAT'S EXPLOSIVELY POPULAR IN JAPAN.

LEGENDZ 1 The Tornado Comes!

THE NAME OF THE GAME THAT LEADS YOU ON THE PATH TO THRILLING BATTLE IS...

LEGENDZ 1
The Tornado Comes!

THE CREATURES OF LEGEND, STILL SPOKEN OF TODAY...

THE MERMAID, THE WEREWOLF, THE YETI...

IT WAS ALWAYS THOUGHT THAT THEY WERE NOTHING MORE THAN PRODUCTS OF THE HUMAN IMAGINATION.

BUT IN THE EARLY 21ST CENTURY, A DISCOVERY CAUSED BY A CERTAIN ACCIDENT PROVED THAT THEY DO EXIST.

THE DATA FROM THESE CREATURES WERE SECRETLY ANALYZED AND RESEARCHED.

SOME OF THE RESULTS OF THAT RESEARCH WERE USED TO CREATE THE ULTIMATE HOBBY, LEGENDZ.

THE LEGENDZ ARE THOSE LEGENDARY MONSTERS, BUT LEGENDZ IS ALSO A GAME THAT PITS THEM IN BATTLE!!

SOUL FIGURE

THE DATA FROM THE LEGENDARY CREATURES ARE STORED IN HERE.

TALISPOD

WHEN THE SOUL FIGURE IS SET INTO IT, THE LEGENDZ ARE REBORN. PLAYERS CAN RAISE THEM AND USE THEM FOR BATTLE.

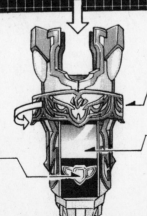

■ JOGSWITCH

HAS THREE SETTINGS: REBORN (BATTLE), SOUL FIGURE (RAISE) AND EJECT (OFF)

■ MONITOR

DISPLAYS THE LEGENDZ'S DATA AND THE RESULTS OF BATTLE

■ SWITCH

SELECT/CANCEL BUTTON

I GOT MY WEREWOLF AS A BIRTHDAY PRESENT. IT'S MY PRIZED POSSESSION.

OF... OF COURSE I DO!!

DON'T YOU LOVE YOUR OWN LEGENDZ?

YOU CAN DO IT!

YEAH!

BUT...I ALWAYS LOSE THE BATTLES, AND I NEVER HAVE ANY FUN.

I WANT MY GUY TO WIN SOMETIMES.

WEREWOLVES DON'T RECOVER THEIR HIT POINTS UNLESS THEY'RE IN AN EARTH-WORLD SETTING.

FIRST OF ALL... THERE'S YOUR ENVIRONMENT.

AAAAH!! NO!

YOU PUT HIM IN A FIRE WORLD!

CHIK

UM... LIKE THIS?

SLAP

IF YOU RAISE IT WITH A LOT OF TLC, YOU'LL BE ALL RIGHT!!

I'LL TEACH YOU SOME TRICKS.

THIS IS HOW YOU DO IT...

DEKAI

BLIP BLIP

LEVEL UP!

BEEEEP

IT'S TRUE— WHEN YOU TAKE CARE OF IT, YOU START FEELING MORE AFFECTION FOR IT.

ALL RIGHT! NOW I'LL FEED HIM!

MY WEREWOLF JUST LEVELED UP!!

HEY!! SHUN-SUKE!

HEH HEH...

LOOOM

DOOOM

HO... HOSUKE...

Flinch

GYA AR

FWip

Y... YEAH.

I HEARD YOU LOST TO RIRIKO YASUHARA AGAIN TODAY. THAT RIGHT?

HEY...

!!

GRAB

DUMMY!!

AAAH!!

KA-DA

KEEP IT UP, AND YOU'LL NEVER BE GOOD ENOUGH TO REPRESENT YOUR CLASS.

IF WE DON'T GET INTO THIS NEXT TOURNAMENT TOGETHER, YOU'RE GONNA MAKE ME LOOK BAD!!

GRAB

YOU'RE THE YOUNGER BROTHER OF THE GENIUS LEGENDZ WIELDER HOSUKE DEKA!!

BUT...BUT... I JUST STARTED HAVING FUN RAISING MY WEREWOLF.

I WANNA BATTLE WITH MY OWN LEGENDZ...

?!

YOU'RE GONNA TAKE RIRIKO'S LEGENDZ TOMORROW!! THEN YOU CAN USE IT IN THE TOURNAMENT!

YOU GOT THAT?!

Ghostly Go Games!

A MAJOR HIT IN JAPAN THAT HAS INTRODUCED A NEW GENERATION OF FANS TO A 4,000-YEAR-OLD BOARD GAME.

AN AWARD-WINNING WRITER AND AN AWARD-WINNING ARTIST TEAM UP TO CREATE AN EXCITING NEW STORY!

- **Volume 7 available in July 2006!**
- **$7.95**
- **Three times yearly**

SHONEN *JUMP* GRAPHIC NOVEL

Story by **Yumi Hotta** Art by **Takeshi Obata**

Supervised by **Yukari Umezawa (5 Dan)**

volume **1**

Welcome to a strange world where an ancient board game can wreak havoc on people's lives! Hikaru Shindo is a regular middle school student who doesn't like to do his homework. Pair him up with a centuries-old spirit named Sai and you're in for some unbeatable Go-playing! Hikaru always thought Go was for geezers, but he's going to discover a new appreciation for the game—with plenty of help from Sai.

Game 1: Descent of the Go Master

UT
MP

UMF...

HEY, LOOK AT THAT...

DON'T BE DUMB. THIS IS A GO BOARD.

A FIVE-IN-A-ROW BOARD.

BET I'LL GET A LOT OF MONEY FOR IT! ANTIQUES ARE POPULAR THESE DAYS, YOU KNOW.

AND IT SURE DOES LOOK OLD. GRANDPA MUST'VE USED IT A LONG TIME AGO.

BESIDES, I NEED THE MONEY. MY PARENTS CUT OFF MY ALLOWANCE 'CAUSE I ONLY GOT 8 POINTS ON THAT SOCIAL STUDIES TEST.

DON'T WORRY!

WIPE WIPE

ARE YOU SURE IT'S ALL RIGHT? I MEAN, MAYBE YOU SHOULD ASK--

DARNIT! WHY WON'T THIS STAIN COME OUT?

NO, IT'S NOT!

BUT HIKARU, IT'S PERFECTLY CLEAN

?

8 points...

WHY DIDN'T YOU STUDY?

RIGHT HERE!!

HERE!

WHERE!?

WHERE?

LOOK, RIGHT HERE! LOOKS LIKE AN OLD BLOOD STAIN OR SOMETHING...

THAT'S WHAT I'VE BEEN TRYING TO TELL YOU!

You can see it?

HUH?

You can... hear my voice?

I JUST DON'T SEE ANYTHING, HIKARU...

You can really hear what I am saying?

.....

WHO'S THERE?!

GRANDPA, IS THAT YOU? STOP PLAYING GAMES AND COME OUT!

AKARI SOMEONE'S UP HERE...

At long last...

At last...

YOU'RE FREAKING ME OUT.

STOP IT, HIKARU!

SHUF

GULP

To the gods, I offer my gratitude...

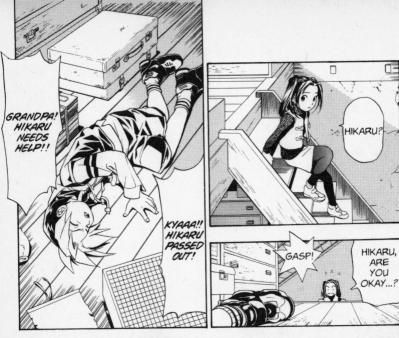

GRANDPA! HIKARU NEEDS HELP!!

KYAAA!! HIKARU PASSED OUT!

HIKARU?

GASP!

HIKARU, ARE YOU OKAY...?

YOU'RE INSIDE MY HEAD...?

W-WHO ARE YOU...?

That is correct. I am inside your consciousness.

C-CON-SCIOUS-NESS?

Hmm... Questions about history!

GASP!

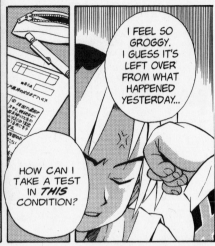

I FEEL SO GROGGY. I GUESS IT'S LEFT OVER FROM WHAT HAPPENED YESTERDAY...

HOW CAN I TAKE A TEST IN *THIS* CONDITION?

IS THERE A PROBLEM, HIKARU?

......

......

I TOLD YOU NOT TO COME OUT!!

GRRR!

AND AN AMBU-LANCE TOOK HIM TO THE HOSPITAL.

HE FAINTED YESTER-DAY...

HIKARU'S NOT FEELING WELL TODAY...

UMM... EXCUSE ME...

IT'S ALL YOUR FAULT!

OKAY, EVERYONE! BACK TO YOUR SEATS!

KLATTA-SKOOT

YOU GOT TO RIDE IN AN AMBULANCE?!

NO WAY!

THAT'S SO COOL!

SO...

WHAT'S YOUR NAME, ANYWAY?

I am Fujiwara-no-Sai.

WEIRD NAME...

WHAT'S YOUR STORY?

I *TOLD* YOU, DON'T TALK TO ME UNLESS I TALK TO YOU FIRST!

MY CONSCIOUSNESS IS *MINE!* I'M NOT GOING TO LET YOU HAVE IT!

GOT IT?!

Yes...

BAM

But, I was only trying to--

During the Heian Period*, I held a position in the capitol as Go instructor to the Emperor.

*Heian Period: 794-1185

HEIAN PERIOD...?

GO INSTRUCTOR ?!

One day, he approached the Emperor with a suggestion...

In addition to myself, there was one other Go instructor.

It was such a happy time for me, I was able to play Go every day...

SO, WHO WON THE GAME?

I SEE...

Let us play a game to decide who shall keep his position.

Sir, I believe that you have need for only one Go instructor.

Everyone's attention was drawn to the board, it was only by mere chance that I saw it...

The game was dead even...

A single white stone lay in my opponent's Go bowl.*

*A container used to keep a player's stones

...I lost the game...

Would my soul be allowed to depart this life and enter nirvana?

No...

My yearnings were strong, I wanted to play more Go...

To add insult to injury, my reputation was irreparably tarnished... I was banished from the Capital for my alleged treachery. With no other skills, no way or reason to live, I threw myself into the river...

.....

HAH! A PITIFUL EXCUSE!!

MMBLE

MMBLE

WH-WHAT ARE YOU SAYING?! THAT IS WHAT YOU JUST DID WITH A WHITE STONE!!

I REFUSE TO BELIEVE THAT EITHER OF YOU WOULD COMMIT SUCH AN UGLY OFFENSE IN MY PRESENCE.

NOW, ON WITH THE GAME!

SILENCE! ENOUGH!

.....

Upset with the turn of events, I was unable to calm myself down...

ON WITH THE GAME, INDEED...

HEH HEH...

!

YOU SCOUND-REL!

And just when I was about to call him on his foul--

I SAW WHAT YOU JUST DID! YOU PUT AN EXTRA BLACK STONE IN WITH YOUR PRISONERS!

FWISH

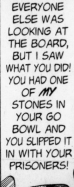

EVERYONE ELSE WAS LOOKING AT THE BOARD, BUT I SAW WHAT YOU DID! YOU HAD ONE OF *MY* STONES IN YOUR GO BOWL AND YOU SLIPPED IT IN WITH YOUR PRISONERS!

I SAW YOU!

WHAT?!

He waited for an opportune moment...

This, of course, has nothing to do with game play. A player need just explain the situation and return the misplaced stone to his opponent's Go bowl. However, *that* scoundrel...

To have one of your opponent's stones mixed in with your own is highly unusual, but on occasion, it *has* been known to happen.

...and then he placed the stone in with his prisoners...

YOU MEAN, HE CHEATED?!